Echoes of the
BIG FOUR

R. J. BLENKINSOP

Published by:
Oxford Publishing Co.
8 The Roundway
Headington
Oxford

PREFACE

With just over 10 years to go before the end of steam on British Railways, this second volume in the series of the 'Big Four' covers a period when all the express locomotives of the main groups were still hard at work and the run-down was only a bad dream. Special trains were being run in profusion for the enthusiast societies, many of those delightful branch lines were active and perhaps most of all the public used the trains for the purpose for which they were designed.

If you are a railway enthusiast there is a fair chance that you will prefer one of the 'Big Four' and this allegiance is also probably due to the part of the country in which you spent your formative years. Watching the trains go by is a sure way of becoming afflicted by the history, layout, design features and love of the local line. I am endeavouring to put that matter right in these books and there are roughly the same number of prints from each region.

Today we grumble at the cost of travel and 20 years ago it was just the same—could I afford to motor over to Grantham to spend a day by the N.E.R. mainline? and as often was the case the answer came back loud and clear—No. So, yet again down to the old faithful which was only two miles away to see the Western engines going about their business. This was a shame as in my collection I have twice as many Great Western shots as all the other lines put together. I endeavoured to put this right at the time but it just was not possible mainly due to family commitments and the distances involved. However, 1958 saw a well worthwhile journey to the south west and my favourite branch line the Axminster and Lyme Regis. Here, if ever there was perfection, ran a line with motive power of pure delight, kept in an immaculate condition and running through some of the best country in England.

I was captivated by it, regret that I only went there twice and that it was not preserved for posterity—thank goodness that one of the Adams tank engines is still running on the Bluebell Railway.

A constant companion in my travels was the largest paperback ever produced, namely "Bradshaw", and like the present B.R. timetable ran to over 1,200 pages. It still makes splendid reading and if you are a bad sleeper like me the problem of getting from Swansea to Bishop Auckland on a Sunday is excellent mental activity in the middle of the night! But of course to take the best pictures in the light available during one day did require a lot of careful planning and timetable study.

The other requirement was good map reading and fortunately at this time the map makers were not so infatuated with motorways and the railway always appeared in a bold black line, so different today when you are lucky if they are shown at all.

I always tried to record the details of each picture and all my negatives are filed away in albums with an index at the front. The index is vital and where possible contains the number of the engine, the location, the train being worked and perhaps most important of all, the date. Without this information it would have been impossible to write the captions with any degree of accuracy.

Today we are being inundated with nostalgia of the 1930s and 1940s both in life style and music—take the Glenn Miller revival for example. The Steam Movement is the same with all types of activity in the preservation of the steam engine in its various forms. This is good for a number of reasons but surely the most important is to let us appreciate the enormous strides we have made in technology. This particularly applies to railways and I know which means of transport I prefer to use in travelling from say Coventry to London. (Of course, it must be electric!)

I hope you enjoy browsing through these pages and that they will bring back some happy memories for you.

1 No. 6011 **King James I** with the 17.10 Paddington-Wolverhampton is travelling over 70 m.p.h. as it descends the bank between Fosse Box and Leamington Spa. Taken on a fine summer evening with sun behind the camera, the driver can be seen standing on the far side of the cab and the fireman sitting and waiting for the down distant signal to come into view.

25 June 1956

2 The cutting here has been filled in and little trace of a railway can be seen. Through the bridge is the estuary of the River Dee with the Welsh mountains behind. 2-6-2T No. 40101 climbs away from Neston South with a local train from West Kirby to Hooton.

31 July 1956

3 Newton Abbot had a stud of 'Manor' class engines to assist trains over the gradients between Aller Junction and Plymouth. The up *Cornish Riviera Limited* is shown entering the tunnel at the summit of Dainton Bank hauled by No. 6010 **King Charles I** and assisted by No. 7813 **Freshford Manor**. Engines employed in banking freight trains from both directions would use the double slip points to return to Newton Abbot or Totnes.

4 August 1956

4 An up morning express from Plymouth is seen passing through Plympton station at the foot of Hemerdon Bank hauled by No. 7814 **Fringford Manor** and No. 6906 **Chicheley Hall**. Gas lamps are visible on the platform as well as the signal box which as a vantage point, gave a wonderful view of the trains.

6 August 1956

5 In the afternoon storms swept in from the Atlantic and the visibility from the top of Hemerdon was poor to say the least. However, I could not resist this one as it was slipping all the way up the 1 in 42 and only near the top did it get its feet properly. Consisting mainly of North Eastern stock No. 34032 **Camelford** of the 'West Country' class is in charge.

6 August 1956

6 As a final gesture to the poor weather I stopped in a lane near the foot of Hemerdon Bank and as luck would have it the sun shone through the clouds at the right moment. No. 7809 **Childrey Manor** and No. 7036 **Taunton Castle** pass with an up express.

6 August 1956

7 Cornwood station the following morning, a very rural scene with 0-6-0 PT No. 3675 passing through with a pick-up freight from Plymouth. The station flowers are in full bloom and passengers are waiting the arrival of a stopping train to Totnes.

7 August 1956

8 Whilst the summer services produced more trains to photograph the external appearance of the engines suffered from lack of cleaning as is shown in this picture of the down *Cornishman* near Bishopsteignton running along the River Teign. No. 6873 **Caradoc Grange** and No. 5071 **Spitfire** have a light load of eight coaches.

8 August 1956

9 Super power indeed, ten coaches and two 'Castle' class locomotives running along the seawall just before turning north at Dawlish Warren station. No. 7029 **Clun Castle** and No. 5089 **Westminster Abbey** provide a fine sight on an up train as storm clouds gather and the sun slips behind an overcast sky.

9 August 1956

10 'Battle of Britain' class Pacific No. 34049 **Anti-Aircraft Command** joins the Western region main line at Cowley Bridge Junction with a stopping train from the Barnstaple line or perhaps it originated from Plymouth via Okehampton. The engine is carrying a Salisbury shed plate.

9 August 1956

11 A picture taken at Shrewsbury shed just before the Wainwright 4-4-0 Class D No. 31075 set out for Towyn with a Talyllyn Railway Preservation Society Special. Inspector Holland is standing on the left with the shed foreman on the right and No. 4942 **Maindy Hall** is partly hidden in the background.

22 September 1956

WELSHPOOL
JUNCTION FOR
SHREWSBURY, STAFFORD,
BIRMINGHAM, LONDON
TRPS SPECIAL
31075
31075
SPL
14

12 The T.R.P.S. special has now arrived at Welshpool and both engines take on water. Dean Goods 0-6-0 No. 2538 is the train engine but perhaps the standard Harris Tweed jackets and grey flannel trousers of the enthusiasts are of more interest!

22 September 1956

13 A 'King' in full flight starting the climb to Hatton alongside Warwick gas works. On the up line the through train from Birkenhead to Ramsgate is passing as No. 6007 **King William III** has just emerged from under the Cape road bridge with the 09.10 Paddington-Birkenhead.

3 November 1956

PNX759

14 I have included this picture to show the old type of refuse collection vehicle with crew taking a rest from emptying the bins. Probably it would qualify as a vintage commercial vehicle today. The local train will have come from Birmingham behind 2-6-2T No. 4112 and has just crossed the A41 out of Warwick. **16 February 1957**

15 A cloudless winter's day with a deserted summit of Hatton Bank. 2-6-2T No. 6116 heads a local train for Leamington Spa and No. 5035 **Coity Castle** with leaking inside cylinder glands comes up the gradient with the down *Cambrian Coast Express*. **16 February 1957**

6011
25
40

16

This train carried through carriages from Birkenhead to Paddington. No. 6011 **King James I** came on at Wolverhampton with a departure time of 11.35 and it is shown accelerating out of Leamington Spa and past the G.W. shed on its way to London, stopping at Banbury.

2 March 1957

17

With the coming and going of mainline trains from the platforms off the picture on the right, the suburban trains were hardly noticed as they crept away from King's Cross and into the first tunnel. Class N2 0-6-2T No. 69577 is fitted with condensing apparatus and shorter chimney for working on the Metropolitan lines to Moorgate.

23 March 1957

18 The next seven pictures were all taken one afternoon that I spent alongside the G. N. mainline just north of Welwyn Garden City. Class B1 No. 61200 is leaving the station with a semi-fast train most likely for Cambridge.

23 March 1957

19 Coming up to London from the north is Class A1 No. 60139 **Sea Eagle** returning to its home shed at King's Cross. Lack of exhaust on this warm spring day was made up by the sight of this beautifully clean engine as soon as it was seen emerging from Welwyn tunnel in the distance.

23 March 1957

20   A black and white picture can hardly do justice to the sight and sound of this train which was audible long before it came into view. The three cylinder A3 Pacifics are unique as a musical experience and No. 60044 **Melton** is living up to its reputation with a down Leeds express—just look at that exhaust!

23 March 1957

21   In the late afternoon a fully fitted freight used to appear behind an express engine on its way north. This seemed to be a regular working and with rattling four wheel wagons swaying from side to side behind its enormous tender No. 60007 **Sir Nigel Gresley** is definitely out of place on this type of work. Note the state of the track on the down slow line.

23 March 1957

60800
90559

22 It was my intention to only photograph No. 60800 **Green Arrow** which was slowing for signals on the up fast line. However a very clean 'Austerity' 2-8-0 No. 90559 was coming along the down slow line, so with a dash along the embankment both trains were included, but as you can see the shutter was fired a fraction of a second too late.

23 March 1957

23 A pair of articulated coaches are behind the tender of Class A1 No. 60120 **Kittiwake** as it thunders through Welwyn Garden City station with a down express. Of more interest is the Class L1 2-6-4T arriving at the platform with water pouring out of the tanks as the brakes are applied too quickly.

23 March 1957

24 Class B17 No. 61671 **Royal Sovereign** enters Welwyn Garden City with a train from Cambridge. This locomotive was often used for hauling the Royal Train and was shedded at Cambridge where it was kept in fine mechanical and external condition.

23 March 1957

25 Southcote Junction looking towards Reading with the mainline to Exeter and Plymouth disappearing out of the picture on the left. 'King Arthur' class No. 30780 **Sir Persant** passes by with a through train from the north to Bournemouth Central.

13 April 1957

30780
399

26

It was unusual to see such a clean locomotive on an up freight train but I think
No. 46152 **The King's Dragoon Guardsman** was running in after a major over-
haul at Crewe works. The location is
looking down from the bridge which
carries the A53 over the mainline at
Whitmore station.

20 April 1957

27

This day was spent looking at L.M.S. engines starting at Whitmore and ending at
Edge Hill. It was a lovely sunny day and
Class 5 No. 45060 is seen leaving Chester
with an excursion along the North Wales
coast. These locomotives, I feel, look
photogenic from whatever angle the picture is taken.

20 April 1957

W561
45060
45060

45527

28

The long deep cutting with its arched supports gives away the location of this picture, it must surely be Liverpool Lime Street, but no signs of electric traction here. No. 45527 **Southport** emerges into the sunlight with a train from Euston, carefully observed by the engine number collectors on the platform.

20 April 1957

29

The other end of the cutting merges into Edge Hill station and this is an evening train coming up the steep gradient behind No. 46114 **Coldstream Guardsman**.

20 April 1957

30 As I have mentioned before in my Western Region Albums, Cup Final day was always important in the photographic diary as many special trains were often required and without the vandalism which takes place today. Just to the south of Rugby, at Hillmorton, the early Wolverhampton to Euston train has been strengthened and has the addition of a Class 5 at the front. No. 44914 acts as pilot to No. 45643 **Rodney** as they head south with fifteen coaches.

4 May 1957

31 Some minutes later two specials pass on their way to Wembley. On the left is B.R. Class 5 No. 73092 which will travel via Northampton, and on the right 'Patriot' class No. 45528.

4 May 1957

32 On the left you can see the wireless masts of the B.B.C. Rugby transmitters and 2-6-2T No. 41285 is propelling an auto train stopping at all stations to Northampton.

4 May 1957

33 A picture full of interest at the south end of Rugby station. In the background can be seen the station and also the bridge carrying the Great Central mainline to Marylebone. G2 0-8-0 No. 49447 has used the flyover on the Northampton line to cross over to the south side of the station and it is so dirty that you cannot see the steam dome cover. With another Cup Final special Class 5 No. 45257 heads for Wembley.

4 May 1957

34 At the junction near Rugby No. 7 Box the line from the north swings round to join the original line from London to Birmingham. Today there is a flyover to avoid the situation shown in this picture where the Class 5 on the left has to be held at signals to allow a train from the north to have priority. The Class 5 is on a special from Birmingham to Wembley and No. 46122 **Royal Ulster Rifleman** will no doubt be getting there first.

4 May 1957

35 Another lucky shot, but I had been hoping for a clean engine on the down *Royal Scot* as was usually the case. No. 46241 **City of Edinburgh** passes No. 7 Box and on the left is G2 0-8-0 No. 49342 slowly heading for Rugby station and the south.

4 May 1957

From time to time I have difficulty in remembering the exact location of some of these pictures as they were taken up to nearly twenty years ago. The G2 0-8-0 is making good progress on its way north to Shrewsbury and I think the bridge in the background carries the A472 down to Pontypool, and yes I have failed to record the number of the engine.

18 May 1957

37

Now we are at Pontypool Road and No. 5004 **Llanstephan Castle** passes a goods yard with a through Manchester to Cardiff train. Note the loaded coal wagons on the right of the picture, a scene which has drastically changed today.

18 May 1957

38   I seem to be very lucky in the number of pictures showing two trains passing each other and here is another example taken in the eastern outskirts of Newport. No. 5918 **Walton Hall** heads for the Welsh capital with a train from Bristol and approaching is W.D. 'Austerity' No. 90323.
18 May 1957

39 Nearing the end of its working life, as it was withdrawn in 1960, the Brown-Boveri Gas Turbine passes Twyford Box with the early morning Bristol-Paddington express. It had a short life, originally ordered by the Great Western Railway, and put to work in early B.R. days during the spring of 1950. I can recall many visits to Sonning Cutting near Reading and hoping for a 'Castle' on the 'Whistlers' working but even so sense prevailed and I built up quite a good set of pictures.

11 June 1957

45613

40 Now we have a change to the north of England as a few hours were spent by the main line at Shap after a holiday in the Lake District. My only visit to Shap and alas I did not have time to get to know all the positions for the best photographs. Late one evening a freight came up with No. 45613 **Kenya** piloting what looks like an 8F 2-8-0 and a banker at the rear of the train.

26 June 1957

41 The following day on our way south we stopped at Hest Bank station to see the up *Caledonian* pass through behind No. 46242 **City of Glasgow**, the locomotive badly damaged in the Harrow and Wealdstone accident on 8 October 1952. Note the water troughs beyond the footbridge.

27 June 1957

42 Farther south at Chester the same day I saw the evening rush hour out of the city and this included a nice clean Class 5 No. 45235 heading westwards into the sun and down the coast to Llandudno.
27 June 1957

43 Weaver Junction where the Liverpool line leaves the mainline to the north and No. 46253 **City of St. Albans** hauling 15 coaches carries the headboard of the up *Red Rose*, which was the late afternoon express from Liverpool to London.
28 June 1957

46228

44 In the evening I motored up to Moore Troughs just south of Warrington and saw a number of expresses from the north. No. 46228 **Duchess of Rutland** gives the track a further soaking as it picks up water—the water tower being clearly visible in the background.

28 June 1957

45 Following the Perth express shown in the previous picture, the next train came from Blackpool and makes a fine sight in the low sunshine behind No. 45653 **Barham.** At this period the coaches were painted maroon but, as in this photograph, there were examples of the old red and cream livery still in use.

28 June 1957

46 About a month later I spent a useful afternoon near the mouth of Welwyn North Tunnel and had the opportunity of seeing and hearing some of the eastern engines. A pullman car train is seen approaching behind an unrecorded engine and in the foreground after much running I managed to get No. 60853 on a down express.

47 For those of you who know the three cylinder Gresley engines well, the next two pictures do not really require any comment. V2 No. 60975 comes out of the tunnel with an express from King's Cross.

20 July 1957

48   A little nearer the tunnel mouth this time and A3 Pacific No. 60056
Centenary bursts into the sunshine heading for Leeds.
20 July 1957

49   The object above the cab of No. 60029 **Woodcock** is a short signal post
and I had hopes that the engine would cover it as it went by, but you
invariably find out when it is too late. The train is from Scotland
nearing the end of its journey.
20 July 1957

50

Class L1 2-6-4T No. 67745 slows down for a stop at Welwyn North station and is framed by a convenient set of signals.

20 July 1957

51

This view is looking north west at Welwyn viaduct and shows an empty stock working headed by an A3 Pacific. It gives a good idea of the size of these magnificent brick built structures which are a continual source of interest.

20 July 1957

52 A photograph which always will give me a lot of pleasure and I call it my 'Tiger Moth' picture as an aeroplane of this type is visible just above the fourth coach. We are looking south east and the A3 Pacific, with firehole door open, heads for King's Cross.

20 July 1957

53 No. 46242 **City of Glasgow** and shedded at Camden is still on the *Caledonian* working shown previously in picture No. 41. In this case it has just passed through Bulkington station with the evening northbound train.

1 August 1957

54 I used to spend frequent weekends with my wife's parents who live near Chester and this has always given easy access to the Midland Region of B.R. This cloudless day started at Chester with a view looking over the road bridge by the station. Note the smoke coming from an engine leaving the Northgate station and no less than eight other locomotives visible as a train leaves for Shrewsbury behind No. 7922 **Salford Hall**.
3 August 1957

55 After a quick drive down to Whitmore on the North Western mainline, I was in time to see the down *Comet* come round the curve behind No. 45644 **Howe** on its way from Euston to Manchester.
3 August 1957

45546
W456

56 In the opposite direction on a special working was unrebuilt 'Patriot' No. 45546 **Fleetwood** with the fireman leaning out of the cab after some work with the shovel, the effect of which is beginning to show from the chimney.

3 August 1957

57 One of the fascinations of watching trains on a summer Saturday in the steam era was the sheer quantity of express working that passed by. On this stretch of the line there was practically a train audible all the time and the four tracks were in constant use. No. 45545 **Planet** comes past with a Birmingham to Glasgow express.

3 August 1957

58 You may be surprised to see yet another shot of No. 46242 **City of Glasgow** but at that time it was kept in good external condition, painted in maroon livery, and was out most days of the week. Here it has just passed under the A53 with Whitmore station in the background and is hurrying south with a Glasgow express.

3 August 1957

59 Now I have moved half a mile north to the water troughs and these two Class 5 locomotives appear to be having a race on their way towards Stafford. On the left is No. 45287 and on the right, a real coincidence No. 45288. I bet that has never happened before!

3 August 1957

60 This is the best angle for the 'Royal Scot' class to be photographed and No. 46111 **Royal Fusilier** has just breasted the summit on the climb out of Crewe with a heavy load of fifteen bogies.

3 August 1957

61 In the evening I called in to a spot overlooking the racecourse at Chester with, in the foreground, the bridge carrying the North Wales line over the River Dee. At this time there were not too many Compounds still working but I was lucky to see No. 41119 in a respectable condition, passing the racecourse set up for the Agricultural show.

3 August 1957

62 And so back to base at Leamington Spa with the 09.10 Paddington to Birkenhead passing underneath the Grand Union Canal which forms the dip between the station and the start of Hatton Bank. Usually worked by a 'King' class engine on this particular day No. 7027 **Thornbury Castle** deputises, and it is good to know that it may run again as it is now at the Birmingham Railway Museum.

17 August 1957

63 Stanier 0-4-4T No. 41902 passes Radford Brewery with the 07.30 Leamington Spa to Napton and Stockton. This train I have photographed many times as we met every morning while on my way to work in Coventry.

21 August 1957

41902

64 At the end of August I spent part of my summer holiday in Devon and I am including three pictures all taken on the same day. No. 1016 **County of Hants** in immaculate condition has just passed Dawlish station with the 08.00 Plymouth to Crewe, changing engines at Shrewsbury. The double chimney does not look too bad in this shot but generally I feel the Counties were not improved when they lost their single chimney.

29 August 1957

65 Starting its journey up the estuary of the River Teign No. 6385 has a stopping train from Exeter to Newton Abbot and has just left Teignmouth. Note the polished safety valve bonnet and the clean appearance even in the height of the summer services.

29 August 1957

66 It is not all that easy to obtain pictures of trains with a clear seascape in the background but this is one such spot between Dawlish and Teignmouth where the line runs by the sea and one can climb up the embankment. No. 34061 **73 Squadron** has a local train stopping at all stations between Plymouth and Exeter.

29 August 1957

67 You may think that this is deep in Southern territory but it is not—in fact the main Great Western line from Paddington to Plymouth is shown just to the south of Reading West station. Two 'King Arthur' class engines are passing with trains between Reading and Basingstoke. No. 30771 **Sir Sagramore** is in the foreground and No. 30785 **Sir Mador de la Porte** approaches from the south.

7 September 1957

30785
30771

68

Another Southern engine leaving Reading West station with a through train from the north to the holiday resorts on the south coast. In this case it is No. 30783 **Sir Gillemere** with quite a mixture of coaching stock from the Midland and Eastern Regions.

7 September 1957

69

On the way home I spent an hour at Goring watching the engines picking up water from the troughs. No. 2845 has a set of empty stock both Midland and Western Region and its A.T.C. shoe can be seen just skimming above the water in the trough.

7 September 1957

70 In the depths of winter No. 60008 **Dwight D. Eisenhower** has just passed through Welwyn Garden City with the down *Flying Scotsman* and starts a downhill run for the next few miles.

11 January 1958

71 No. 34054 **Lord Beaverbrook** approaches Vauxhall station with a lightly loaded train and a Southern E.M.U. is about to overtake.

12 April 1958

791
32487
32487

72

The driver of this engine looks incredibly small leaning out of the cab as No. 32487, an 0-6-2T introduced in 1897, is on its way to the carriage sidings with a load of empty stock from Waterloo station.

12 April 1958

73

Quite a cheerful smile from the fireman of this pannier tank leaving the goods loop to the south of Ruabon station. The engine, No. 7403, has a guard's van in tow and will be at once turning right at Llangollen Junction where the line to Dolgellau leaves the Shrewsbury to Chester mainline.

26 April 1958

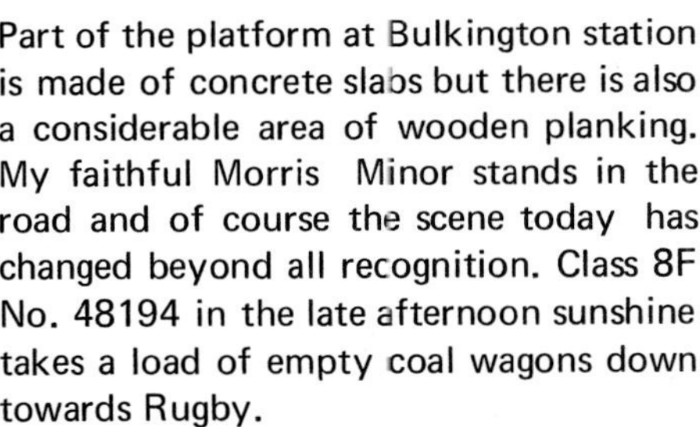

74

Part of the platform at Bulkington station is made of concrete slabs but there is also a considerable area of wooden planking. My faithful Morris Minor stands in the road and of course the scene today has changed beyond all recognition. Class 8F No. 48194 in the late afternoon sunshine takes a load of empty coal wagons down towards Rugby.

6 May 1958

75

1958 was to be the last time that I managed to take a holiday by myself and the aim was to see some more of the working between Newton Abbot and Plymouth, but most important of all the Axminster and Lyme Regis branch of the Southern. I started off early to spend an hour at Steventon and this picture is of No. 70024 **Vulcan** with the up *Capitals United Express* on the fast stretch shortly before Didcot.

19 May 1958

WINCHESTER
CITY
82014

76 And then on to Winchester, still a very dull day, with a standard 2-6-2T No. 82014 passing through the city station. I wonder if the large rack of bicycles is still in use on the down platform?

19 May 1958

77 Unfortunately I was not here when City of Truro was working this line and on the day in question No. 76064, a standard 2-6-0, came off the G.W.R. branch at Shawford Junction, onto the relief line, with a train from Didcot to Southampton Terminus. In the distance above the tender of the engine can be seen Winchester Cathedral and over on the right St. Catherine's Hill.

19 May 1958

30028

78 We pass the sight of Stockbridge station every year when we go on holiday and it is difficult to believe that I took this picture so many years ago judging by the scene today. Class M7 0-4-4T No. 30028 stops with a push-pull set on its way from Andover.

19 May 1958

79 After an overnight stay in Salisbury I went to the Tunnel Junction to see the early morning express leave for Waterloo headed by No. 34009 **Lyme Regis.** The line in the left foreground, complete with check rails for the sharp curve, comes in from Southampton.

20 May 1958

80

This will be a semi-fast to Basingstoke and beyond, taken from the A30 road bridge and looking north-east. 'King Arthur' class 4-6-0 No. 30452 **Sir Meliagrance** makes its way into the misty morning.

20 May 1958

81

Class N 2-6-0 No. 31813 comes under the road bridge with a train of weed killer wagons, a guard's van being inserted at each end.

20 May 1958

73050
DZ 6480

82 I should like to think that this is the Pines Express on its way from Bournemouth but with the time at around 11.30 I feel it is unlikely. Anyway, it makes a good picture as it passes Henstridge station hauled by standard class 5 Nos. 73050 and 73051. Fancy scrapping that nice Austin 7 pick-up!

20 May 1958

83 Motoring on to Sherborne, I took three pictures from the roadbridge carrying the A352 into the town. This must be a Salisbury to Exeter stopping train and hauled by 'Schools' class No. 30903 **Charterhouse.**

20 May 1958

84 With the 'Schools' class disappearing into the distance, the 10.30 from Exeter to Waterloo approaches Sherborne behind No. 34072 **257 Squadron**. The up line is about to be re-laid and you can see the new flat bottom rail lying along the edge of the sleepers.

20 May 1958

85 I expect experts on Southern working can identify this train which has just pulled away from Sherborne station on its way to Exeter. No. 34011 **Tavistock** has a load of 12 coaches and a 4-wheel parcels van.

20 May 1958

A meeting outside the south portal of Crewkerne Tunnel, another example of the game of luck. The coal allocation in No. 34029 **Lundy** seems to be a bit on the spartan side and No. 34078 **222 Squadron** has steam to spare.

20 May 1958

87

And now we come to the object of the exercise and what a glorious sight it is—Adams Radial Tank No. 30582 in polished black livery and one coach. My favourite branch line from Axminster to Lyme Regis—alas no more. The train is about one mile out of Axminster.

20 May 1958

10
30582

88 I went to a different spot for the next return working in the afternoon but again not far away from Axminster and as you can see the day has turned out to be magnificent.

20 May 1958

89 Between the workings of the branch I went to the foot of Honiton Bank and caught this 'Merchant Navy' class No. 35029 **Ellerman Lines** on a midday train from Waterloo to Exeter.

20 May 1958

90 The last trip down the branch in the evening was hopefully to have a request smoke effect but it did not produce much to liven up the picture. Note the cans of oil above the buffer beam, and the engine is just at the foot of the incline which will take it up and over the mainline to head down towards the south coast.

20 May 1958

91 No. 7017 **G. J. Churchward** leaves Totnes with the 07.30 Truro-Paddington and running without any assistance over the Devon banks to Newton Abbot. What a profusion of telegraph poles and wires on the up side of the line, and note the tarpaulin on the side of the goods shed keeping out the weather. A 2-6-2T waits in the station for the next freight to bank up Rattery incline, see picture No. 18 in *Reflections of the Great Western*.

22 May 1958

6004
6123
BAY TOR
BOARDING KENNELS

92 Sweeping round the curves into Teignmouth, No. 6004 **King George III** is working the 09.40 Falmouth-Paddington. Rather a cramped sight for photography but the magnificent sky and clean engine help the picture. The chimney has now been demolished.

26 May 1958

93 *The Shamrock* was one of the three titled trains to serve the London-Liverpool route and this is the up train on a Saturday morning when it left Liverpool at 08.20 and arrived at Euston at 12.18. The motive power is No. 46210 **Lady Patricia** in green livery and it is seen near Stableford.

14 June 1958

94 And so we finish this Volume with another 'Princess Royal' class locomotive, but in maroon livery and soon after passing Whitmore. No. 46207 **Princess Arthur of Connaught** carries the headboard of *The Merseyside Express* departing Liverpool 10.10 and arriving London 13.45.
14 June 1958